THE SECRET LIFE OF AN IBIS

Written by: Rickey Taing
Illustrated by: Thic Leng

authorHOUSE

AuthorHouse™
1663 Liberty Drive
Bloomington, IN 47403
www.authorhouse.com
Phone: 1 (800) 839-8640

© 2018 Rickey Taing. All rights reserved.

No part of this book may be reproduced, stored in a retrieval system, or transmitted by any means without the written permission of the author.

Published by AuthorHouse 10/22/2018

ISBN: 978-1-5462-6402-6 (sc)
ISBN: 978-1-5462-6401-9 (e)

Print information available on the last page.

Any people depicted in stock imagery provided by Getty Images are models, and such images are being used for illustrative purposes only.
Certain stock imagery © Getty Images.

This book is printed on acid-free paper.

Because of the dynamic nature of the Internet, any web addresses or links contained in this book may have changed since publication and may no longer be valid. The views expressed in this work are solely those of the author and do not necessarily reflect the views of the publisher, and the publisher hereby disclaims any responsibility for them.

"The Secret Life of an Ibis"

With this piece I share with you the epics of my life. For those who went through life's tragedies, those who have lost loved ones, those who are hurt, those who have healed or are healing, I share your voice. This poetry is dedicated to humanity. May future generations learn from my generation and the generations before mine. Your ancestors' voices echoed in this poetry.

Be forewarned, as your eyes move across each line, and with the turn of each page, some of you may be scraping the scars of your own life.

Rickey Taing

Epilogue

Ibis is a Cambodian national bird that is shy and smart in nature, according to tradition.

The collection of poems is a reflection Rickey's life. From 1975-1979, nearly two million Cambodians were decimated by the horrendous Pol Pot regime. Those years of torture did not break but strengthened him. The rumdul flower's essence is floating in the air, conjuring his memories. These poems are his stories from childhood to manhood. It is his discovery of life while he was forced to relocate from country to country and camp to camp.

1

A-leurk, a-leurk, in the dawn, a-leurk, a-leurk in the dusk
The curtain unveiled
Ibis grazing the field
Shots went off, you screeched in despair
A-leurk, a-leurk, you cry in the dawn, as if to warn
A-leurk in the dusk, searching your youngsters
Leeches bound onto your feet
Crickets, snails vanish
Tree tops are bare
The sky your blanket
Emptiness everywhere
Bullets astray, your tears unnoticed
Nearly fifty years you reappeared
I hear that you live in the North, Tmatboey village
Mythical you seem to be
One hundred pairs remain
Don't be afraid, come from your hide
Your land is small, but you have a place
Come, come and claim your place.

2

"Rumdul Khmer"

Gentle breeze in the evening
Fragrance fills a lover's mind
On your branch you sway in the wind
Tantalizing young hearts
Your leaves frolicking lonely bees
Your ovary soothes hunger
Your shape, plum
My heart glows, my eyes gleam
Rumdul Khmer
Men are spellbound by your potion
Hahhh...
Seeing you, holding you once
A lifetime memory
Thousands of miles away
The rumdul's aroma is in my inhalation.

*Rumdul flower: Cambodian national flower

3

Revolution

The land is dry
The crops are not producing
Drought, drought everywhere
Mama, we are hungry
No rice in the pot
Dad, the cows are sick
Revolution
Join the Khmer Rouge regime
No more rich
No more poor
Learn to read
Equality for all
Come, fill your belly
Revolution
All youths, come join the regime
Live the prosperous lives you were given by rights
Remove the leeches and parasites
Chase the foreigners out of the motherland
Revolution
Before I realized, I was knee deep.
Blood shed everywhere.
Rivers and lakes, red in color
Revolution…
Children starving, mothers and fathers killed
Revolution for the love of my country
Revolution has betrayed my love.

4

Don't write me down in history that you have conquered me
A slap across my face with your evil hand was a gentle breeze
Did you expect me to fall on my knees and beg for mercy?
Think again—for my body you may bruise
But my soul has ascended.

5

Don't stare me down with your slanted mouth
Small almond eyes
My lips are busted
My body scrawny
Belly larger than a melon
But my mind is wholesome
Flick me off like a nuisance mosquito
But I will return
Did you think that your hands thrashing in the air,
Mouth foaming, lessen my dare?

6

Gra-ma wrapped around his waist
Old rusty rifle pointing
One by one man and child plead for breath
"Leeches of society!" you shouted
Did you know that I was there to catch you from your mother's womb?
If a leech I am, then it is you who benefited from my blood.

*Gra-ma: Light, thin, towel

7

Why?
Over two scores now you remain to torture me
I thought I had left you
Our encounter was bitter
My father and sister you erased
Yet you are not pleased
Why do you insist on haunting me?
Go; go to your grave!
I now rest in the Buddha's palm.

8

Dark skinned, thick lips, chinky eyes
Combat boots, gra-ma around his head
Old, rusty scythe on his left
Know no life, know no love
Leading a group of men tied to a rope
Disciplined
One foot after another
Orderly
Hoping for mercy
Awaiting grace
Like the disappearance of kouprey
One by one history has erased you.

*kouprey: Cambodian national bovine species.

9

Yesterday he asked
Look after my mother and son
I shall be back
But don't expect me
I am too educated to breathe
Ung gha needs me to help lead Cambodia
Your face was sad
Your skin bruised
Your ribs I can count all
Do you realize how awesome your life is?
Very soon you will be free
When the rope tightens around your neck.

*Ung gha: Pol Pot regime

10

"Cruelty thy name"
The earth was dry
The winds are gone
Not even a snake would dare to slither
A woman crying, pleading for mercy
Husband stood by, afraid to make the slightest move
Eight devils each took their turn
From noon 'til morning her spirit gone
Eyes white, subdued to raging hormones
Husband forced to approve
Witnessed the horror, he too cried like a baby
White sac between her thighs, as it bathes in blood
Jhea yo Ung gha, Victory to Ung gha.

11

Two sheets between her teeth she bit
Fear of being heard, sound is choked
Life between her legs, body on the earth
She quickly cleaned and dried
Afraid of being captured, the hand over its mouth
Sound no more
Life starts with an end.

12

Sister...Jie

Your long slender arms
Flailing in the air
Gently tapping my hair
You whispered,
"Jie loves you"
Fanning me with your bare hand to chase the mosquitoes
Yet, you are nearly lifeless
"Jie will protect you" I remember hearing you while I am nearing sleep
My armor ceased no more breath
Yet I feel you are here.

*Jie: Teo Chao dialect for older sister

13

You, thin and scrawny
Crawling between two cows
Digging up potato roots
Three you dug up
Fear of danger
The tame beast kicked you
Your mouth foaming, holding tightly onto the roots
"Mama, cook them" you pleaded
"Oun, you take one, give me to your niece
Nibble on it slowly"
Your breath shallow
Your eyes white.

*Oun—Khmer for younger brother or sister

14

Cornfield
Teasing each corn by its husk
Hand trembling in fear of getting caught
I left my footprint on the earthly mud,
Leaving a trail for Ung gha scouts to follow
A rifle pointed at my back for being hungry
"Traitor!" shouted a boy no older than nine
"How dare you steal from Ung gha!"
I pleaded for mercy, before I realized, my head by his feet
Dragged to the senior scout, awaiting my sentence
The heavens provided mercy
I get to live to face another day of hunger.

15

Once I heard that you were around
Out to the movies, out to gamble
The war came
Again, you were estranged
Three fish you caught
Broiled on a stick
Sister and I salivated
You ate your fish alone
Hunger pain visited, like a ghost asking for its soul
I cried to the air
I know mama cared
I know mama cared.

16

"Third Brother"

Your body developed
Your muscles toned
Almond eyes, tender flesh
Out of the nest you were forced
A paddle swatted against your back
"Ou…" you cried
The revolution near an end
You tended to your mother and youngsters
A stick on your shoulders, you balanced family clothes
Pots and pans you gathered
Mines set off, yet you were calm
Each of your siblings, you brought to safety
A living angel you are to me
This gratitude I owe you.

17

In one trail, we marched
Pots and pans clanking
Children crying
Feet were blistering
Day blended into night
Rain turned earth into mud
Bombs bursted
Perhaps another limb
Perhaps another body
Someone's child vanished
All for the taste of freedom.

18

"Camp"

My home new, yet unfamiliar
The earth carries me
The scent, strange
Lost in the world
Mountain breeze calms my fear
No smell of blood in the air
Lake water, nice and fresh
Freedom is near
But my home is afar
I yearn in the dawn, to hear ibis
Calling her children home.

19

Sipping a brewed cup of Oolong tea
Sitting by the window
Leaves dancing to the rhythm of the wind, raindrops chinking
On the metallic roof
I hear you calling, "let's play kick the can."
Uncombed hair, grubby face, dirty nails
You tender soul
This is what I remember most about you
Your dreams unrealized
Your eyes puffy when you learned that your
puppy was sacrificed for the men
Last I heard you were deported from Kao I Dang
It is in my loneliest times that our fondest
childhood memories keep me sane.
I whistle.

*Kao I Dang: Thailand refugee camp

20

A young boy called me
"Mister, remember me?"
"Who are you?" I asked
"Look deep down here you will see," he said
Searching in the dark I see not the boy
"Help me"
The voice only heard, the face not made
"Look deep down here you will see"
Troubled, I closed my eyes
"Can you see me now? Look deep down here"
A young boy in ripped shorts, shirtless
--trembling and crying
"You have forgotten me."
"No, no, you have always lived in me"
Time has lapsed, this body is feeble, but I have carried you all along.
I pray to the Buddha for wisdom and compassion for you all along.

21

Back in the day, I grew in haze
No water was needed for this plant
Wild as the dandelion
Light and frayed
Plucking off the feathers of a chicken, I clucked
But I must go on.

22

Autumn in the evening
Spring in the morning
Drinking wine in the midst of dawn
Suddenly I realized I miss my hometown.

23

Come, impregnate yourself with my blood
And tell her it's from me
For this is as close as I can ever be
You parasitic beast, how is it you fare better than me?

24

"Flea"
Go and inject her
Leave my saliva and secretions
Be gentle and leave no scars
Then come back and bite me
Go; go on your way!

25

This morning your fragrance in the air
I searched for you but I see you not
Something about this fragrance that reminds me of you
I have always wondered.
How have you been?
I remember clearly by the river the night you departed
I suppose you are not coming back to me
Your scent ephemeral
Until this morning you came back,
This time in the air.

26

I rowed my boat to catch your glimpse
Under the crescent moon
By the river
Gentle breeze flirting the oars
Handkerchief embroidered in golden thread
Your tender hands lightly caress my lips
In secrecy we meet
Reality sets in when your dad discovered
You are the reflection of the moon, teasing the river
Your touch short-lived
Class has separated us.

27

Little bird, why do you taunt me?
You fly in the rain gracefully
You seem to be free
Do you know what worry is?
I suppose you can ask me
"Are you enjoying your tea while I am seeking shelter"?

28

Looking in the mirror
I see the scar running on my back
All from the banana I attempted to steal
As I lift this pen, the wound dehisces
Haunting memories rushing to share
I heard a young boy yelling in the dark
Afraid of the skull in the backyard
Hunger jabbed every inch of me
Two crickets in Mama's fist
I survived to carry this scar.

29

Two hands as one
The Buddha above my head
Knees on the earth
I succumb to life
The Buddha, my teacher
The dharma, my boat
The sangha, my oar
How insignificant I am.

30

Strive to live a life filled with wisdom, rather than greed and power
Morning dew quenches thirst
Lotus petal shields its pollen.

31

Protect the mind, as a guard dog protects its master.

32

Spring cedes to Autumn
A torrential rainstorm exposes the bamboo roots
Hiding under the straw roof, the moon appears lonely
Grasses yearn to grow, weeds malnourished
Breathing quietly in the musty cell
Morning dew quenches my thirst
Falling leaves cover the roots
Branches naked
It is then that I have awakened to realize that I am part of the elements
Dharma wheel, it is my nature.

33

Traveling along the path to discover myself
Buddha is within me.

34

Cicadas chirping melodiously
Mayflies do not know their end
Life comes and ends
This is the path of samsara.

35

Hold still and watch as the breath
Becomes ephemeral
It is then will you know living from dying.

36

"Tears in the dawn of autumn"
Cicadas buzzing tunes of change
Lovers find melody in the atmosphere
Mayflies glowing without realizing their surrounding
Cows wagging off their tails
Crickets chirping, as if to warn
The moon reflects over the serene Mekong River
Looking up to the stars, my hometown disappeared
My bones are creaking, lines are drawn on my cheeks
This skin has become sinewy
Where have I disappeared to?
"I" am not me
All of "me" made "I".

37

The path to discovering the self is to master the mind.

38

Some people say memories are painful
I say memories are saviors
They connect the past to the present
They strengthen you
Like a "cow that pulls the cart"
The wheels go 'round and 'round
How can they hurt, if you are numb?

*Buddha's teaching

39

I am many pieces that make me whole
Your uterus, my home
It is because of our ancestors that I am here
Your body a medium
A piece of cloth you carved out
Crying in the dark you heard me
Your tender hands pulled me from the bottom
to meet eye-to-eye
It is then will you realize your ancestors are within you
This life, a cycle—birth and death are one
This life I am your child,
next life you're mine.

40

I remember when you entered
Your eyes wide open
Your cries loud
Not sure why you closed your eyes then
Or did you know
Your skin tender, your grasp gentle
Rosy cheeks, gentle smiles
Puckered lips, as if to speak
Did you want to warn me?
Your laughs, gentle purr
Your walk was clumsy
But you never ceased to try
When you call me Lao gu
My heart pounded, fluttered like a butterfly caressing a jasmine flower
Who knew that today I am old
Who knew that I am old.

*Lao gu: Great-uncle (Teo Chow dialect)

41

"Death"
When death comes to me
I will ask, what took you so long?
Have you lost your way?
Man trembles when he hears you are near
This sagging skin, weary eyes
Shall enjoy your company
Take this paddle and row for now
Heaven is not ready for me
But when the time comes, my servant, you will free me.

42

"Mama's teaching"

Sitting by the porch
Deep in gratitude
Mama and I reminisced
Lesson in life begins
Spider spun its threads on the rose tree
"Have you ever wondered about the life of a spider?"
"No" mama
"When it was young, it had siblings
As it matures, no siblings, no family
In its web, only it remains
No friends. It is the master of its own faith.
It looks out of its own window, neither wind, rain, nor sun bothers it.
It is determined to live
At the end, we are alone.
When the storm of life comes
Stand firm!"

43

This life of mine empty and free
Pleasure neither here nor there
Searching for 'something' but found nothing
The feet are free, the mind is trapped
Chicken searching for a nest to lay eggs
I am just as unsettled
Soothing in meditation, I submit to the dharma
A learned man will know
It's futile to dominate the external,
it's the internal that must be subdued.
I pay my homage to the "Om".

Made in the USA
Middletown, DE
16 November 2018